BEFORE YOU CLIMB THE BUSINESS LADDER TOO

(An e-Course)

Learn business basics before and after start up.

Ogaleap Business
iBootCamp 1.0

James O. George

BEFORE YOU CLIMB THE BUSINESS LADDER TOO

(An e-Course)

Learn business basics before and after start up.

Ogaleap Business
iBootCamp 1.0

James O. George

BEFORE YOU CLIMB THE BUSINESS LADDER TOO

Ogaleap Business iBootCamp 1.0 Copyright © 2020

Copyright © 2020 – James O. George – All rights reserved.
A Ogaleap Business iBootCamp Publication

All rights reserved. No part of this book may be used or reproduced by any means, graphic, electronic, or mechanical, including photocopying, recording, taping or by any information storage retrieval system without the written permission of the author except in the case of brief quotations embodied in critical articles and reviews.

<u>Note</u>:

Because of the dynamic nature of the Internet, any web addresses or links contained in this book may have changed since publication and may no longer be valid.

Ogaleap Book Services Email:
lionelheapower@gmail.com

Call/SMS/WhatsApp:
+234(0)-902-238-1935

BEFORE YOU CLIMB THE BUSINESS LADDER TOO

TABLE OF CONTENT

DEDICATION

INTRODUCTION
What iBootCamp is VERSUS What it isn't

UNIT 1:
STARTING A BUSINESS IN YOUR 20s AND YOUR 30s

UNIT 2:
STARTING OR DOING A BUSINESS WHILE AT A FULL-TIME JOB OR WHEN YOU WANT TO MAKE A CAREER CHANGE

UNIT 3:
GOING INTO BUSINESS WHEN YOU'RE OUT OF WORK; AND HOW TO KNOW WHETHER YOU'RE READY TO BE AN ENTREPRENEUR OR NOT

Ogaleap Business iBootCamp 1.0 Copyright © 2020

DEDICATION

To everyone hungry to learn more about building a successful startup for their business.

We are in this together!

INTRODUCTION
WHAT IBOOTCAMP IS VERSUS WHAT IT ISN'T

As we begin this e-Course, it is very important that your mind is in the right place. This will help me balance your expectations properly.

Are there expectations you should have from this iBootCamp? Yes there are. In fact, we will see some of the objectives and goals of this e-Course as we kick-off.

So, What is iBootCamp and what is it NOT?

1. iBOOTCAMP e-Course IS a comprehensive breakdown into a guide. That's why it's called a course. We aren't giving you one idea but possible options to help you discover your own idea and work with it.

It ISN'T a "make 6 figures in 1-year" blueprint

2. iBOOTCAMP e-Course is a fail-proof system that will require you to put in the work in order to produce your own results .It ISN'T a "get rich quick" scheme.

HOW DO YOU PREPARE AND GET THE BEST FROM BUSINESS IBOOTCAMP 1.0?

Pay close attention during each session and take notes from major points.

Write down your questions that are "practical" to you and "relevant" to the topics. **See you at the top of this ladder mate.**

BEFORE YOU CLIMB THE BUSINESS LADDER TOO

UNIT 1:

STARTING A BUSINESS IN YOUR 20S AND YOUR 30S

If you are in your 20s and you desire to be an entrepreneur, you are doing yourself and your future a whole lot of good.

So, congratulations on making this great choice to start your own business at a young age!

Do you know why I'm congratulating you?

Most business-people are usually at least 35 years old when they start a business, but there is no reason you can't be successful or even start earlier. In fact, the earlier a you decide to start climbing the ladder, the better it will be for you.

If you're heading to 20 or just past 20, that means you were born into technology unlike those before you.

What's the upside of this?

As a person who was born with technology at their fingertips, there are so many options for you. Can you believe that! You have more options than someone who was born in, say, the 80s or 70s. Now, you can take advantage of technology because it makes a lot of things easier for you.

For instance, you can start what we all call the "side hustle". I know you've heard of that especially with the current global pandemic lockdown and the most recent internet explosion (thanks to covid19, everyone is now selling something).

You can start a side hustle, something via technology, something you may not have had the time or flexibility or even the resources to do physically.

Or still, you can start a full time business. Maybe you'll create the next "YouTube sensation," or start a digital marketing agency, or become a social media influencer, and so on. The possibilities are truly endless.

Permit me to say that, the world really is at your fingertips today if you're in your 20s.

Kudos to our 20s folks! "Indomie Generation" or not, you've got a huge advantage.

However, in order to climb the business ladder, it's not free, neither is it cheap. You may need to make some sacrifices.

Do I still have your attention?

1. Stop Playing too much (all the time)

I really hope you won't crucify me on this one. But just stay with me and you'll understand better.

You don't have to give up all your fun, but the truth is, partying every weekend, driving/strolling around with your buddies all day, playing video games, pursuing the latest clubs, gambling or sporting 24/7 is not the way to create a successful business - at least not in the beginning when you're doing a lot of the work yourself that you can later outsource (believe me, starting out is the part that needs your attention and more work than you realize).

So, you have to cut them to minimal so you can focus. Alright? If you skip this one, you'll struggle with a lot of things that will get in your way. And believe me when I tell you, all the strength you have is meant for what counts not for unnecessary things or else you will wear out.

Have you realized that many times, you've gathered ideas but you've either lost them or been too distracted to focus on building them? Check some of your reasons, you will see that most weren't even worth it.

2. Get some Financial Education

Let's face the facts a little: how good are you with financial management regarding saving, investing, selling and earning while still carrying out your responsibilities as a person? Your present financial status will tell us that.

You need to educate yourself in finance, both business, and personal. There is a lot of information that you likely don't know. There are a lot of financial questions you don't even know how to ask to get the right answers. When you don't even know what questions to ask, it puts you in a dangerous situation. Instead, accept that there are things you don't know yet and educate yourself about them.

It's not a bad thing that you don't know. But it is a bad thing that you don't know and you aren't doing anything to change that nor willing to do anything about it.

So, calm down and educate yourself financially.

3. Explore Ideas

As a learning hub, we are putting together various systems that will help you achieve this. Joining our eAcademy or network will give you that opportunity. So stick around to the end of this course to learn how to join.

How do you explore ideas?

Don't forget, we are still talking about the things you need to do in order to start climbing the business ladder in your 20s.

Let me beg you: don't just start business because you attended one online class and the speaker told you how he or she made 6figures in 7days as a business person. You aren't the same. Sure the strategy may work for you, but check your starting point. Are you fully equipped with the idea that will begin your launch?

A dear friend was just complaining the other day (and I'm sure you have noticed it too) that everyone on WhatsApp, Facebook, Instagram is selling something or trying to teach people how to sell something. Some are real and some are fake. But it's becoming too much and many people don't even know what they are doing. Some start and lose interest and enter another one. Can you imagine within 6 months, Uncle Sam has posted more than 10 different products for sale from shoes, to cars, imports, phones, clothes, cakes, fries too?

You almost want to ask him, *"Uncle Sam, please what are you selling?"*

You have to learn to know what idea you want to develop and be know for providing value for.

How do you do this?

Make a list of your ideas that fit in with your skill set or things you'd like to learn. Take a course, find a mentor, or get a business coach to help you get started faster. Doing the research beforehand is better than jumping right in. Give yourself a few months to explore all possible ideas. *Again, I said, don't be like Uncle Sam.*

4. Write a Business Plan

Let me ask you this, *"Do you have a business plan at all? What do you think a business plan is?"*

Someone will say it's a drawing board. Well so, but it's a bit more complex than that. Everything we have talked about so far is what will lead to that.

I mean, once you are set on your idea, write a business plan. Check out our e-library, the internet, college, or university for classes, workshops, and more regarding starting a business to get some assistance.

Once you have chosen a business and have the plan, that means you've investigated all aspects and are ready to start. Set your intention by putting all tasks and actions in a calendar for you and anyone on your team (you will grow o, so prepare for them). Then do the steps and start the business. You will be so happy you did. By the time you're 35, you'll have an established business while your friends are just getting started.

Our next point will be on starting a business in your 30s. But even though you're in your 30s, I know you've started grabbing value from this first session already. And that doesn't mean the next session won't be helpful for those in their 20s either.

STARTING A BUSINESS IN YOUR 30S

If you're in your 30s and considering starting a business, there must be a big reason to make you want to do it. You may be unhappy in your job, or you may enjoy what you do so much you want to start your own firm. Starting a business in your 30s puts you in good company, though, since most people start a business around the age of 35 (just like we saw above).

In your 30s, you've likely already had a lot of experience and education in something that is causing you to be filled with the dream of entrepreneurship. It could be based on what you are doing now, but it might be something totally unexpected.

Maybe now you have kids too, and you realize that the old job doesn't give you the time freedom that you need, and you feel as if you're missing out on your kids' lives. So, you set up a business the entire family can work in. Whatever your reason, it's a great time to start a business. So, congratulations to you too!

Some great business ideas for people in their 30s are software companies, digital ad agencies, and so much more. To come up with the right business for you, ask yourself what you're trying to achieve. It always begins with you, please.

How do you want your life to look once the business is established? Do you want to be location independent, or do you want to start something in your local area? Do you want to earn millions, or are you fine with six figures?
All these factors matter when choosing the right business for you.

So, let's dive in: How can you support yourself while you start this business?

It's important to know how you can do it financially and be successful. You likely already have a mortgage and other bills to contend with that you didn't have in your 20s. Make a budget. Cut back, tighten your belt, and jump in. Look to your business plan to determine what you need.

You may want to consider asking the following questions before starting your own business too:

1. Am I really leaving a stable job for this?

If you know you have savings and can finance your start-up, it may cross your mind that you are nuts to leave a stable job. And plenty of people will tell you that very thing without you even asking. But is a job really that stable? What makes it stable? Won't the jobs you create also be considered stable jobs for someone or others too?

2. What about your training, experience, and knowledge, are they all irrelevant now?

You may think you're wasting it, especially if you're going in a new direction. But who says you must do the same thing forever? Why can't you change your life if you want to? If you've been in corporate finance since you graduated college at 22 years old but now you want to start a software firm, you'll use some of the skills, but it's different enough to give you a change if that's what you desire.

3. Will this business, if successful, give me the results I desire?

Before picking the business you are going to run (*probably for at least the next 10 years*), make sure it's really what you want to do, and that is how you want to live your life. Imagine a day in the life of you establishing this business, and what a day in that life will be like once the business is well established.

You can literally start any type of business you want to in your 30s. There are very few barriers to entry for any type of business other than resources. Do you have the funds, skills, and ability to do it? If you do, go for it.

UNIT 2:

STARTING OR DOING A BUSINESS WHILE AT A FULL-TIME JOB OR WHEN YOU WANT TO MAKE A CAREER CHANGE

If you have a full-time job but you desperately want to be an entrepreneur today, you can do it if you pick the right type of business.

This is the tricky part. Don't make the mistake of picking just any business while you're still at your 9-5 because you might put yourself at risk. Accept it, you still need your 9-5 that's why you're there. Don't go and listen to one motivational speaker and then throw your 9-5 away when you have nothing to fall back to.

But it's very possible to work and still build a good business for yourself, no matter your day job. I highly recommend doing a digital business. You can design digital business so that you don't have to do it during specific hours or times which allows you time to do your day job, attend to family and do other things conveniently.

For example, if you decide to start a blogging business and make money as an affiliate marketer, it doesn't matter when you create your content; if you publish content that your audience wants to see regularly, they'll still respond.

So, if you're interested in starting a business when you're already in a full-time job, here are some ideas to try out:

1. **Virtual Assistant**:

A Virtual Assistant is kind of like a virtual/digital secretary. You can set up your own Virtual Assistant (VA) business to work in such a way that you are not available on call. You can have your clients assign work by a certain time for you to finish by a certain time. All they should care about are the deliverables, that is, your delivery.

What I mean is, you start your VA business, get clients who need to get things done (that's what a secretary does which gives you the leverage of having more than one client too since it's all digital and you can be worlds apart and not be affected) to give you their tasks to finish with certain hours that suits you.

Many managers, celebrities and co are hiring virtual assistants now for their private lives especially those working from home. Some could be to remind them of things like working out, meeting with an appointment, and so on. It's not really much if you're good at it and disciplined enough to commit too.

So, you can do this and still be on you 9-5 job too, no loss and you're building little by little for the big target. Cool, if you ask me.

2. **Digital Marketing**:
If you start a digital marketing agency, you can easily do it while you have your full-time job due to software that enables you to schedule actions. So, on the weekends when you're off, you can feed ten emails into your auto-responder plus ten blog posts into your blog schedule, and it'll work for you all week.

Thanks to Facebook, Instagram and Twitter ad managers, you can help people do digital marketing or you run yours for affiliate products all week at a price. Every weekend, you check it out, make adjustments and updates and set it up again. It's a good way to earn and sell automatically too, still, without affecting your 9-5.

Everything I'm sharing with you are actually practical and timetested by people and it works. So, if you feel you'll do them well, you can try them too. Don't just know it, nod and do nothing, please.

Seek for, pick one and take an action!

3. **Blogging**:

Personally, I've run my own blog via self education more than through learning which didn't give me the speed as I'm supposed to. However, I found out that blogging isn't only for people with passion to write alone but people who have passion to share and serve others too.

For instance, there are travel bloggers who enjoy travelling, taking photos and simply sharing their experiences with people who are interested. Do you know that there are many of such who now travel for free, lodge in hotels for free and shop for free, why, because those sponsors want this popular blogger to give amazing recommendations via photos and videos about their business to the world. It's a very easy form of marketing and advert that will remain on that website as long as it is functioning.

I didn't say you should go and become a travel bloggers o. There are others like fashion bloggers, food bloggers, book bloggers, faith, medicine, insanity, music and the list is endless (blogging is another issue for another day)

I strongly recommend you use www.wordpress.com for your blog since they have both free and paid plans that you can work and build with. As a blogger, you can create the content for your blog whenever you have the time. The system will schedule the blogs that you set up to be published regularly. No one will realize you wrote it at 2 am or that you wrote all ten blog posts in a series in a weekend. You make money via ads and products that you recommend in your blog.

Although, it will need time to develop, it pays you well over time and develops your personality, communication, etc.

4. Graphic Design Firm:

If you are good with Photoshop and other software that enables you to design beautiful graphics (from web banners to book covers), then you can start a graphic design firm. If you build websites too, that's even more than your firm can do. Hire some help, and you have a real business that can go far. CANVA app has made it easier to do on your Android phone now without any prior experience too.

I've personally earned a few bucks doing designs for people myself. I just had to pause a little lately because I needed to give more attention to my coaching classes.

5. **Create an Online Course**:

What's your knowledge and experience worth? Do you know how to do something that is super-cool and useful? Or, maybe it's not even useful but other people want to do it?

If so, you can create a course. Today, there are software or sites available like *www.Teachable.com* or *www.aMember.com* or *www.thinkific.com* that enables you to deliver courses without you even being there. **Thinkific**, for example allows you to even create a few courses free of charge which you can sell to people.

Courses are cool but they should be things you have good knowledge of not just anything you want to sell. So, what are you good at that you can teach? If none, then I suggest you start learning more about your passions and become a Master there.

6. **Become a Writer**:

You can start a writing business by becoming an author and selfpublishing via Amazon and Kindle, Kobo books, etc. or you can actually write as a service for other businesses that need content for their websites, ads, and brochures.

This is another cool way to do business why you still retain your job.

7. Outsourcing Firm

I put this last because it's easy and hard at the same time. Outsourcing is one of the topmost office-less agency. I like to call it the *linking business*.

Let's say I have contacts who love to buy clothes and would go extra lengths to get them. They even ask me if I know sellers or whatever. Now, it's not wise to tell them no. I'll lose both an opportunity and through away another person's paycheck. What I do is I tell you, in fact, I am selling. The person may be surprised but I'll tell them, don't worry, I am a business man. What I do is this, I'll look for any other contact who is good at that same thing too or someone else who is and tell them I have a job for them. I don't have to link them, I act as seller to one and act as buyer to another. The only thing I may supply is the real owners address for delivery purposes but payments will pass through me. So, I can collect a little extra for that service and pay the seller while I keep the change. The buyer gets deliveries, they are happy and the seller is too. And I am happy and richer even though I didn't go anywhere. What I've done us render service and I got paid for that.

It's a good business but it can land you in trouble if you don't know how to do it and if you go work with an unprofessional seller who provides low quality service.

So, there are many more ideas today that you can do from home even with a full-time job - even if you have kids. The main thing to consider is the flexibility that your business will afford you, and if it has the capability to earn enough money to replace your job or not. If it can't replace your job, you may want to find something else.

What about starting a business when you want a career change? We'll talk about that next.

STARTING A BUSINESS WHEN YOU WANT A CAREER CHANGE

Are you considering starting a business because you dislike your job or you're ready for a career change? If you love the idea of giving up your current career and making a big change to become an entrepreneur, you're in luck because there hasn't been a better time to start your own business. This is it!

Here are a few of my recommendations:

1. Test Drive- Experiment with the market for a while

Don't quit your job right away before you're ready. That's one mistake many of us make and it's the cause of so much unemployment and lack of money in the hands of most skilled people today.

What you need really is to do this right for the maximum chance of success. For example, if you think you want to start a massage parlor or hairdressing salon, but you've not worked in one, you really should try to work in one a few times a week on your time off work, so that you can get a feel for it. Don't leave your job and enter something you have no feel for or experience in. That's a federal highway if you're a learner.

If you want to start a digital job, you can test drive that easily at home via your laptop or device. You can give your idea a try by setting up a Facebook group for people who might want to buy your idea someday. See how much interest you can develop before quitting your job.

The Bible says, *wisdom is profitable to direct, and in the multitude of it, there is safety.*

2. Be Willing to Commit

Sometimes, when you want to change careers, you can get into a big hurry and act too fast. You must, however, remember that, even if you don't like your job right now, it is paying the bills. This is very important. Don't deny it. No matter how small, if it's paying your bills, don't throw it away unless you have a better alternative.

You'll need to be willing to work nights and weekends (or when you're off work) to make your dream come true. But if you are willing to make a commitment to it, you will be successful once your idea is developed.

3. Change Your Mindset

It's hard to think like a business owner when you are still in a job. However, you'll need to change your mindset when you are working on your business. You have to start thinking like an owner who is an expert over a person with a job. You're the one in charge now, so you want to do things your way and the most appropriate way that will eventually lead to success.

4. Replace Your Income before Quitting

This is the cause of so many stranded ideas and innovators today. So many catch ideas but do not consider their stability to sustain it.

You might not have to replace everything, but you should replace the needed portion of your income before you quit your day job to run your business full time. One thing to do is set up a budget. Read about the 50-30-20 budget, which is going to help you ensure you have enough to devote to your business. Get books, read please. I can never overemphasize this issue. You have to like to read books, business books, finance, leadership, motivation and history. They will go a long way. The world's richest men read, so what makes you think yours will be different. And the thing is that we all read. It's either we aren't going for books that interest us or we just don't know what interest us, which is really sad. Do you know how many pages you read online via people's statuses, posts and tweets? You'll be shocked.

You can join my **reading network** if you're interested in changing that, message me privately.

Remember that, the only thing that can hold you back from starting your own business at any time in your life is YOU and only you. If you don't believe in your ideas, it's hard to implement them. If you don't hype it, no one can. One way to believe in your ideas is to study and research your audience and your industry until you become an expert on both.

BEFORE YOU CLIMB THE BUSINESS LADDER TOO

UNIT 3:

GOING INTO BUSINESS WHEN YOU'RE OUT OF WORK;

Ogaleap Business iBootCamp 1.0 Copyright © 2020

AND HOW TO KNOW WHETHER YOU'RE READY TO BE AN ENTREPRENEUR OR NOT

It has been quite a scary year, hasn't it? However, the truth is, no matter how scary this time is or the year has been, this is a great time to start your own business.

I think it's time many of us, with all our potentials and skillset stop seeing ourselves like broke and stranded people when there are hundreds and thousands who are willing to pay for what we have to offer.

Newton's Law of motion is effective here: Do nothing and nothing happens. Do something and something will happen. It's as simple as that.

You can take control of the situation you're in and come out of it better than ever. If you didn't lose your job, you might never be brave enough to become an entrepreneur. People like Mark Cuban, Kathryn Minshew, and even the most powerful woman on Wall Street, Sallie Krawcheck, all started their businesses after being fired. Isn't that amazing? Out of a disappointment, they located their destinies.

Being fired is a common way people end up in their own business, and it can be a very successful way to start. This is mostly because when people are afraid or heavily pressed, the fighter in them responds. For instance, the fear of starvation or losing their home or families, can make people work harder and are much more committed. In fact, many entrepreneurs report being fired multiple times before finally getting the hint and going out on their own.

If you want to start your own business when you're out of work, this is one time you should not delay finding a way to bring in income so you can work your dream. As the world continues to develop, the need for innovations and innovative ideas are growing massively. You are a very fundamental part of the resources that can meet that need. You're more than a consumer, you can start something from where you are right now.

Let's get right into it:
Trust me, money isn't the first... Wisdom and strategy is.

1. Get Something, a Side Hustle, for Support:

If your dream business is not a service-based business and you have to earn money for the product you will be creating, consider starting a service-based business on the side like driving for a rideshare company, delivering groceries, drop-shipping, outsourcing or something like that which won't distract you from your business.

2. Live Off Your Unemployment or the current level of supply you're at:

If you do get unemployment or you have some form of buyout package or a particular support system, you can live off that for a time. Cut all your extra expenses, such as eating out and buying clothing, etc. Stick to the basics while you build the business. The goal is not to look successful but to BE successful.

3. Know Your Skill Set, What are you good at and passionate about:

You should know that you are good at doing. Right now, it is not a time to try to learn something completely new because you are unemployed and need to get money coming in. You can work as a consultant doing what you did before, or you may have to figure out how your skills align with something else.

This is where brainstorming comes in. Ask yourself those hard questions. Get out your pen and paper and take notes. What can I do? What skills do I have? List them. Know yourself and don't be afraid or ashamed to admit you need to learn. There are free or low expense courses all over the internet in different fields. Take them and develop yourself for what you want to be known for. It's not about having a degree but about having a skill that works for you. Got that?

4. What Do You Love?

Is there something you are good at that you really love doing and would do for free if you could? If there is something you get excited about that also has a way to earn income from it and build a business, what would it take to turn that into your business?

Think about that. You can make money from any passion. You just need to know how. There are people who make money taking photos, answering calls, talking, dancing, laughing, saying something funny, dressing up, writing, and so on.

5. What Problems Can You Solve and for Whom?

This is the bottom line. Starting a business must be built on this. You're more than a seller. You're a problem solver. But first you have to know what problems you're taking on and how do you plan on tackling it. When people know this, you'll be the one they come to in order to solve that problem.

Knowing who your ideal audience/client/customer is can help you figure out what problems you can solve for them using your skills, knowledge, and experience.

Everyone has a need. Which of them can you solve. Think deep.

6. Determine How You'll Market Your New Business:

If money is tight, you may have to consider some interesting alternatives to get people to notice your business. For example, you may want to start a blog, or a YouTube channel or an Instagram, or Facebook or even Twitter, depending on which works best for your type of business. Social Media has become the best place to gain a huge business following, sometimes, even without paying a dime for adverting.

With good flyer designs and captions, consistency, you're bound to get noticed by people of interest.

(We have a special social media business hack coming up, where we teach you how to leverage on social media, go viral and turn followers into buyers. Don't miss the information after this Course.)

The main thing to realize is that nothing is stopping you from coming up with a massive moneymaking business idea and building it from today EXCEPT you. Chances are that if you are here reading this, you already have at least a glimmer of an idea of what you want to do. Now you just need to research the idea, study the audience, and match it to your skill set, then implement and execute, and you're going to be a success.

We've given many examples of the benefits of starting your own business.

Now, let's look at the flip side – when you should not become an entrepreneur and how to know you're not ready to be your own boss. Get ready to hear what you've never been told before!

When you should not become an entrepreneur

(*HOW TO KNOW YOU'RE READY OR NOT READ TO BECOME ONE*) We've come a long way and I'm so excited that you made it. However, now's the time to wrap it up with the hard truth you've never been told.

Anyone can but an entrepreneur BUT NOT EVERYONE CAN BE AN ENTREPRENEUR.

There are many reasons why a person may choose to become an entrepreneur, but there are some that tend to be signs that the business idea won't work out so well for the business owner.

Let's look at those reasons you should not become an entrepreneur which are also signs that you aren't ready to be one:

1. You Find it difficult to Commit to your ideas or to anything: If you cannot commit to a "workday" of some sort and a schedule to implement your ideas, it is not going to work out. You cannot make things happen, doing nothing. Remember Newton's Laws of Motion.

If you aren't the type of person who can create a plan and then follow it to completion, a small business might not be for you.

Maybe you want to find a remote job or a flexible alternative. Commitment is key to building any and every idea.

2. You Hate Your Job:

If you hate your job, it's time to go find another one, but that's not the only reason to start your own business. A lot of the things you dislike in your job might exist in the business too. For example, if you are currently a secretary and your boss is on your last nerve, becoming a virtual assistant isn't going to solve that problem because you'll end up with several "bosses." Furthermore, customers can be a thorn most times and if you don't know what you're doing, you might lose it on them.

Don't start a business out of grievance with your old job or boss. Don't start a business to prove a point. Start s business because you want to and because you desire to solve problems yourself.

3. You want to get rich quick without working hard:

If you think having your own business means doing nothing, you've read too many books and fantasies. Even the "Four-Hour Work Week" Guy did not work only four hours a week – at least not at first. There is a joke about being an entrepreneur that goes like this, "Only an entrepreneur chooses to work 80 hours a week because they did not want to work 40 hours a week for someone else."

Deep within this is the truth. You know it's easier to work all night building your own business than another man's. That's the normal human psychology. But starting your own business means you'll work harder than you used to, only this time, you decide when and how you work.

4. You're unwilling to learn, unlearn and relearn:

As an entrepreneur, you're going to have to learn about taxes, finance, and so many things that have nothing directly to do with your business. You cannot just rely on others when it comes to these things. If you are not willing to learn about these things, don't start your own business, because you'll end up failing your first tax year when you owe a ton of money you can't pay.

The world is growing fast and a lot is changing everyday. If you refuse to learn, you'll never grow beyond where you are.

5. Your Spouse or children don't support you:

This particular point is relative but true. There is something about the blessings of a family united together. If that disappears, you aren't going to make it. Communicate your dreams to them, seek their own suggestions, let them see the value and benefits, and let them assure you of their backup. You'll succeed when they are solidly behind you.

If your family does not support you in your dream, it might not be the right time to start. This is true whether you're a stay-athome parent or the breadwinner, because the only way you can be successful in business is if your partner supports you.

In conclusion, If you think becoming an entrepreneur is easier than working at a job, you are wrong! Totally wrong. It's different, for sure, but it's not easier. If you aren't good at being self-motivated, managing finances, and delegating while executing, entrepreneurship might not be for you. However, if you can get on board with what you need to do and do it, you can overcome any personality deficiency if you really want to do it and become a success.

Thank you and good luck!

BEFORE YOU CLIMB THE BUSINESS LADDER TOO

DID YOU ENJOY THIS COURSE AND WOULD LOVE TO BE PART OF OGALEAP LEARNING COMMUNITY AND GAIN ACCESS TO ALL OUR UPCOMING TRAININGS FOR BUSINESS PEOPLE?

BEFORE YOU CLIMB THE BUSINESS LADDER TOO

SEND A WHATSAPP MESSAGE:

"I WOULD LOVE TO JOIN THE OGALEAP LEARNING COMMUNITY"

TO HERE

OGALEAP IBOOTCAMP 1.0 WAS BROUGHT TO YOU BY OGALEAP TRAINING SERVICES, AN ARM OF OGALEAP BOOK SERVICES. WE ARE A KNOWLEDGE HUB DEDICATED TO EMPOWERING YOU FOR GROWTH THROUGH LEARNING, MOST OF WHICH ARE FROM BOOKS.

CHECK US OUT OF OUR SOCIAL MEDIA HANDLES:
FACEBOOK/INSTAGRAM/TWITTER

CHECK OUT OUR E-LIBRARY COLLECTIONS TOO

CONTACT US:
OGALEAP BOOK SERVICES
LIONELHEAPOWER@GMAIL.COM

BEFORE YOU CLIMB THE BUSINESS LADDER TOO

+234-902-238-2935

Ogaleap Business iBootCamp 1.0 Copyright © 2020

www.ingramcontent.com/pod-product-compliance
Lightning Source LLC
Chambersburg PA
CBHW072237230526
45466CB00024B/2091